The Rough Riders at Camp Wood in San Antonio, Texas

Lieutenant Colonel Theodore Roosevelt of the First U.S. Volunteer
Cavalry Regiment — the Rough Riders

Cornerstones of Freedom

The Story of
THE
ROUGH RIDERS

By Zachary Kent

CHILDRENS PRESS ®
CHICAGO

U.S. Army regulars fighting at San Juan Creek near Santiago, Cuba

Library of Congress Cataloging-in-Publication Data

Kent, Zachary.

  The story of the Rough Riders / by Zachary Kent.
    p.   cm. — (Cornerstones of freedom)
  Summary: Describes how Teddy Roosevelt formed the
Rough Riders at the beginning of the Spanish-American
War and led them into battle at San Juan Hill.
  ISBN 0-516-04756-6
  1.   United States. Army. Volunteer Cavalry, 1st—
History—Juvenile literature. 2.   Roosevelt, Theodore,
1858-1919—Juvenile literature. 3.   United States—
History—War of 1898—Regimental histories—Juvenile
literature. [1. United States. Army. Volunteer
Cavalry, 1st—History. 2.   Roosevelt, Theodore, 1858-
1919. 3.   San Juan Hill, Battle of, 1898. 4.   United
States—History—War of 1898—Campaigns.]
I. Title. II. Series.
E725.45 1st.K46   1991
973.8'9—dc20   90-22444
                                                    CIP
                                                    AC

PHOTO CREDITS

AP/Wide World Photos—9 (top right), 16

The Bettmann Archive—Cover, 2, 5, 9 (bottom right), 10
(right), 23, 24 (right), 29

Historical Pictures Service, Chicago—9 (top left & bottom
left)

North Wind Picture Archives—1, 4, 7, 12, 13 (2 photos), 14
photos), 15, 17 (2 photos), 18, 19, 20, 21, 22, 24 (left), 25, 26,
27 (3 photos), 28, 30, 31 (right), 32

UPI/Bettmann Newsphotos—10 (left), 31 (left)

(Cover—Theodore Roosevelt and Rough Riders)

Theodore Roosevelt proudly wears the uniform of a Rough Rider.

Bullets hissed through the humid Cuban air and ripped the dense jungle grass. From the crests of the San Juan Heights, south of Santiago, Cuba, Spanish soldiers poured a withering gunfire down upon their American enemy. At the foot of these two high hills, U.S. soldiers hugged the ground, waiting for orders. Some men clutched at wounds, groaning in pain.

As the minutes passed on the afternoon of July 1, 1898, the ranks thinned. These American soldiers had come to help the Cuban people win their fight for independence from Spain.

Suddenly, from the rear, fresh troops crowded into the battleline. Dressed in blue flannel shirts and khaki trousers, these men were members of the First U.S. Volunteer Cavalry Regiment—better known as the Rough Riders. Although they were cavalrymen, the Rough Riders marched forward on foot. Only their commander was on horseback, excitedly urging his men toward action.

Easily recognized by his pince-nez glasses, gritted teeth, and thick moustache, thirty-nine-year-old

Lieutenant Colonel Theodore Roosevelt had responded swiftly to his orders: "Move forward and support the regulars in the assault on the hills in front." Pushing among the U.S. regulars, the Rough Riders soon reached the foot of the first rise, later named Kettle Hill. A captain waiting there stopped them. The captain said that the line could not advance without proper orders, and his colonel was nowhere in sight.

"Then I am the ranking officer here," Roosevelt answered, "and I give the order to charge."

The captain hesitated but Roosevelt insisted, "Then let my men through, sir."

Sparked by these words, the excited regular soldiers acted. "The whole line," Roosevelt later declared, "tired of waiting, and eager to close with the enemy, was straining to go forward." Out of the cover of the woods and up the grassy slope the Americans advanced, shouting and firing as they ran. The cheering Rough Riders led the way. Colonel Roosevelt, his blue neckerchief blowing in the breeze, galloped in front. The Rough Riders were charging into glory and everlasting fame.

Never before had there been such an unusual outfit of American army volunteers. Western cowboys ran in step alongside New York millionaires. Full-blooded, sharpshooting Indians fought beside blue-

The charge of the Rough Riders at San Juan Hill

blooded Ivy League athletes. But no matter where they came from, they were all proud to call themselves Rough Riders.

"Remember the *Maine!* To hell with Spain!" was the slogan that had plunged the United States into the Spanish-American War in 1898. Since the days of Christopher Columbus, Spain had occupied the island of Cuba, just ninety miles south of Florida. In 1895, tired of harsh Spanish rule, the Cuban people rose up in open revolt.

Two rival New York City newspapers took full advantage of American interest in the war. The *New*

York Journal, owned by William Randolph Hearst, and the *New York World*, owned by Joseph Pulitzer, were in stiff competition to sell newspapers. Both newspapers printed sensational news stories with giant banner headlines and front-page illustrations. Across the United States, people read wild stories of gallant Cuban rebels, cruel Spaniards, and bloody acts of violence.

As the Cuban revolution raged, relations between the United States and Spain grew more strained. In January 1898, to protect Americans living in Cuba, President William McKinley ordered the battleship *Maine* to make a "good-will" visit to Cuba. For weeks the *Maine* rested peacefully in Havana Harbor. Then, on the evening of February 15, 1898, a tremendous explosion jolted the *Maine* half out of the water, hurling metal fragments high into the air. Burned and bloodied sailors shrieked in agony as water rushed into the sinking ship.

Angry Americans blamed the mysterious explosion on a Spanish bomb. "DESTRUCTION OF THE MAINE BY FOUL PLAY," blared the *New York World*. "THE WHOLE COUNTRY THRILLS WITH THE WAR FEVER," trumpeted the *New York Journal*. "Remember the *Maine!*" chanted Americans, demanding revenge. Caving in to public pressure, President McKinley asked Congress to

William Randolph Hearst (above) hinted in the *New York Journal* (below) that Spain was responsible for the sinking of the *Maine*.

Joseph Pulitzer (above) ran stories in *The World* (below) urging American intervention in Cuba.

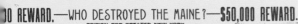

REWARD.—WHO DESTROYED THE MAINE?—$50,000 REWARD.

NEW YORK JOURNAL
AND ADVERTISER.

NEW YORK, THURSDAY, FEBRUARY 17, 1898.—16 PAGES. PRICE ONE CENT.

TION OF THE WAR SHIP MAINE WAS THE WORK OF AN ENEMY.

0,000!

0 REWARD!

**Detection of the
petrator of
aine Outrage!**

Assistant Secretary Roosevelt Convinced the Explosion of the War Ship Was Not an Accident.

The Journal Offers $50,000 Reward for the Conviction of the Criminals Who Sent 258 American Sailors to Their Death. Naval Officers Unanimous That the Ship Was Destroyed on Purpose.

$50,000!

$50,000 REWARD!
**For the Detection of the
Perpetrator of
the Maine Outrage!**

L OFFICERS THINK THE MAINE WAS DESTROYED BY A SPANISH MINE.

a Sunken Torpedo Believed to Have Been the Weapon Used Against the American Man-of-War—Officers n Tell Thrilling Stories of Being Blown Into the Air Amid a Mass of Shattered Steel and Exploding Shells—Survivors Brought to Key West Scout the Idea of Accident—Spanish Officials Pro- test Too Much—Our Cabinet Orders a Searching Inquiry—Journal Sends Divers to Havana to Report Upon the Condition of the Wreck. Was the Vessel Anchored Over a Mine?

BY CAPTAIN E. L. ZALINSKI, U.S.A.

863,956 — The — World. — 863,956

WORLDS CIRCULATED YESTERDAY — NEW YORK, THURSDAY, FEBRUARY 17, 1898 — WORLDS CIRCULATED YESTERDAY

MAINE EXPLOSION CAUSED BY BOMB OR TORPEDO

Capt. Sigsbee and Consul-General Lee Are in Doubt---The World Has Sent Special Tug, With Submarine Divers, to Havana to Find Out---Lee Asks for an Immediate Court of Inquiry---Capt. Sigsbee's Suspicions.

CA T. SIGSBEE, IN A SUPPRESSED DESPATCH TO THE STATE DEPARTMENT, SAYS THE ACCIDENT WAS MADE POSSIBLE BY AN ENEMY

Dr. E. C. Pendleton, Just Arrived from Havana, Says He Overheard Talk There of a Plot to Blow Up the Ship---Cap Zalinski, the Dynamite Expert, and Other Experts Report to The World that the Wreck Was Not Accidental---Washington Officials Ready for Vigorous Action if Spanish Responsibility Can Be Shown---Divers to Be Sent Down to Make Careful Examinations.

The New York World a day after

Theodore Roosevelt (left) as a young man in the Dakota Territory

Captain Leonard Wood (right)

grant him war powers. On April 25, 1898, Congress declared war against Spain amid patriotic songs and wild cheering.

Among the Americans wildly eager to fight were Assistant Secretary of the Navy Theodore Roosevelt and White House physician Leonard Wood. The son of a wealthy New Yorker, Roosevelt was a Harvard graduate, active in politics and public service. Although he was sickly as a boy, a lifetime of vigorous exercise, and three years' work as a rancher in the Dakota Territory, had molded his body into muscular shape. Leonard Wood was a U.S.

Army veteran and an outdoorsman, too. While fighting renegade Apache Indians in the Southwest, the thirty-seven-year-old physician had won the Medal of Honor for his courageous leadership.

For years, Roosevelt had talked of raising a cavalry regiment of frontiersmen. Now, with the outbreak of war, Congress passed a Volunteer Army Bill. One part of the bill called for three new regiments made up of horsemen and riflemen from the Rocky Mountains and the Great Plains.

In early May 1898, Roosevelt resigned his government position and accepted an army commission as a lieutenant colonel. He agreed to organize the First U.S. Volunteer Cavalry Regiment, to be commanded by his friend Colonel Leonard Wood. "Theodore Roosevelt," declared Secretary of State John Hay in surprise, "has left the Navy Department where he had the chance of his life and has joined a cowboy regiment."

Applications to join the new regiment arrived by the bushel. Roosevelt chose his men carefully. "We had a number of first-class young fellows from the East," he recalled, "most of them from colleges like Harvard, Yale, and Princeton; but the great majority of men were Southwesterners, from the then territories of Oklahoma, Indian Territory, Arizona, and New Mexico."

Within days the recruits gathered at Camp Wood in San Antonio, Texas, for their training. The suntanned, rawboned men of the western territories arrived first. "They were a splendid set of men, these Southwesterners," declared Lieutenant Colonel Roosevelt, "tall and sinewy, with resolute, weatherbeaten faces, and eyes that looked a man straight in the face without flinching."

These rough volunteers included gunfighters, gamblers, and bear hunters, Rocky Mountain stage drivers, Colorado silver miners, and Texas cowpunchers. Ben Daniels was marshal of Dodge City,

Shoeing a horse at the camp in San Antonio, Texas

Left: Rough Rider William Pollock, a Pawnee Indian. Right: The regimental mascots: Teddy, Cuba, and Josephine

perhaps the toughest town in the West. Cowboy Billy McGinty never walked as much as a hundred yards if he could ride a horse instead. "Dead Shot Jim" Simpson of Albuquerque, New Mexico, could shoot a jackrabbit at a distance of a thousand yards. From the Indian Territory came Cherokees, Chickasaws, Choctaws, and Creeks—all keen-eyed riflemen and expert trackers. The Arizona recruits brought a mascot—a growling golden mountain lion named Josephine.

A few days later, Roosevelt's hand-picked Easterners arrived. These volunteers from New York

Sergeant Hamilton Fish

Rough Rider
officers (left)
at dinner in the
San Antonio
camp City included the millionaire sons of business tycoons and Wall Street stockbrokers, as well as a few city policemen. The Westerners quickly dubbed these New Yorkers the "Fifth Avenue Boys."

Dozens of Ivy Leaguers soon strode into camp. Many of them had ranked among the best athletes in the country. Dudley Dean was called by sportswriters "the most famous quarterback ever on the Harvard football team." Bob Wrenn and Bill Larned played championship tennis. John Waller was a high jumper at Yale, and Hamilton Fish had pulled an oar while captain on the Columbia crew. These patriotic young men from the nation's oldest families looked upon the war as a stirring adventure.

Many names were suggested for the new regi-

ment, such as "Wood's Wild Westerners," "Teddy's
Terrors," and "Teddy's Riotous Rounders." But the
name that stuck was "Roosevelt's Rough Riders."
For his 1,000 cavalrymen, Colonel Wood purchased
Texas horses, many of them unbroken. The work of
bronco-busting attracted crowds of visitors. The
best cowboys in the regiment rode the backs of
bucking mustangs, giving free shows.

When enough horses could be saddled, drill prac-
tice began. Dashing across the dusty countryside
mounted in military formation, the Rough Riders
had whipped themselves into fighting shape by the
end of May. By that time, however, a U.S. naval
squadron commanded by Commodore George Dewey
had destroyed the Spanish Asiatic fleet in Manila
Bay. The Rough Riders worried that the war would
be over before they had a chance to fight.

The Rough Riders on the railroad trip to Tampa, Florida

At last, their orders arrived. The Rough Riders were to join the United States Fifth Army at Tampa, Florida. The War Department was pushing ahead with plans for an invasion of Cuba. On May 29, Lieutenant Colonel Roosevelt proudly watched the regiment ride to the railroad depot. "In their slouch hats, blue flannel shirts, brown trousers, leggings and boots, with handkerchiefs knotted loosely around their necks, they looked exactly as a body of cavalry should look," he later said.

During the four-day journey to Tampa, people crowded up to the windows and cheered the troops at every stop. "They brought us flowers; they brought us watermelons and other fruits, and some-

Serving rations at Tampa (left). The horses (right) were left behind when the Rough Riders went to Cuba.

times jugs and pails of milk," marveled Roosevelt. At Tampa the Rough Riders pitched their tents beneath the sweltering Florida sun. "On our arrival . . . ," declared Colonel Wood, "we found everything confused and in a most frightful mix. Streets packed with soldiers and a foot deep in real beach sand."

Major General William Shafter commanded the 17,000-man invasion force. A lack of transport ships had caused plans to be changed. The Rough Riders were told to leave their horses behind. General Shafter also ordered that the regiment be reduced to just 560 men. "I saw more than one, both among the officers and privates, burst into tears when he found he could not go," Roosevelt afterwards recalled.

The dock at Tampa. The ships carried the Rough Riders to Cuba.

The 560 Rough Riders cleared to go piled aboard the cramped transport ship *Yucatan* with their equipment and supplies. For two weeks, the U.S. invasion armada of some fifty ships slowly steamed southward. Although it was crowded and hot aboard the transport *Yucatan*, Rough Rider Ogden Wells wrote, "It is very pleasant sailing through the tropic seas toward the unknown. The men on the ship are young and strong, and we are eager to face what lies before us."

At last on June 22 the great convoy reached the

village of Daiquiri on the southern coast of Cuba. Wildly disorganized, the transports swung close to the dock and the soldiers scrambled ashore. Meantime, eighteen miles to the north, American warships had trapped the Spanish Atlantic fleet inside the harbor of Santiago. Now the army planned to march through the steaming jungle and capture that city by land.

The Rough Riders were among the first troops to move inland. "In the open places," remembered Trooper Wells, "the sun was like a furnace and the packs were like lead." "It was a hard march," agreed Lieutenant Colonel Roosevelt, "the hilly

The transport ships coming into port at Daiquiri, Cuba

19

Troops going to the front pass the battle scene at Las Guasimas

jungle trail being so narrow that often we had to go in single file." Some troopers joked that the regiment should be called "Wood's Weary Walkers."

On the morning of June 24, at a ridge called Las Guasimas, hidden Spanish soldiers suddenly attacked. Traveling with the advance troops, reporter Richard Harding Davis later exclaimed, "We were caught in a clear case of ambush . . . the hottest, nastiest fight I ever imagined." Zipping Mauser bullets tore through the dense undergrowth. The rapid fire of machine guns banged loudly through the trees.

At the head of the Rough Riders' column, Tom Isbell, a Cherokee from the Indian Territory, was hit by seven bullets and severely wounded. New York socialite Sergeant Hamilton Fish fell to the ground with a bullet through his body, the first Rough Rider to die. Another shot killed Captain Allyn Capron, and a bullet in the spine paralyzed *New York Journal* reporter Edward Marshall.

Allyn Capron

Crouched in the jungle undergrowth, some angry Rough Riders began to curse. "Don't swear—shoot!" commanded Colonel Wood. The Americans fought back, crashing through the thick jungle and charging up the ridge against the entrenched enemy. "We advanced firing," said Roosevelt, "and drove them off." In that brief skirmish, eight Rough Riders died and thirty-four were wounded. Still, said Roosevelt, "We wanted first whack at the Spaniards and we got it." The retreat of the enemy from Las Guasimas cleared the road north to Santiago.

During the following days, the Americans regrouped and plotted their strategy. When Brigadier General Young fell ill with fever, Colonel Wood took charge of the U.S. Second Cavalry Brigade. "This left me in command of the regiment," declared Roosevelt, "of which I was very glad."

By July 1, the army had pushed forward to the outskirts of Santiago. Blocking the way was the fortified village of El Caney. To the west, the San Juan Heights bristled with barbed wire, trenches, and blockhouses. General Shafter ordered an attack on both El Caney and the San Juan Heights.

The battle began with the fight for El Caney. For hours, sweating U.S. soldiers struggled to capture the village. Cannon roared and rapid-fire Gatling guns spit bullets. Finally, the Twenty-Fifth Infantry, a regiment of black soldiers, charged into the village streets. When the smoke cleared, the American flag waved above El Caney.

The attack to the west began under a rain of Spanish cannon fire. The Rough Riders pushed forward through the jungle and splashed across San Juan Creek. Ahead rose the heavily defended San Juan Heights, with San Juan Hill to the left and Kettle Hill to the right. Waiting for further orders, the Rough Riders crouched along the riverbank and lay in the high grass, while Spanish gunfire cut into the ranks. Captain Bucky O'Neill, former mayor of Prescott, Arizona, strolled up and down the line.

Bucky O'Neill

"Captain, a bullet is sure to hit you!" yelled one of his sergeants.

"Sergeant, the Spanish bullet isn't made that will kill me!" calmly answered O'Neill. One minute later a bullet smashed through his head and he dropped to the ground dead.

Some soldiers fainted in the heat, while others grabbed at painful wounds. "I sent messenger after messenger to try to . . . get permission to advance," Roosevelt recalled. When the orders to advance

finally arrived, the impatient Rough Riders sprang to their feet. But at the foot of the San Juan Heights, their way was blocked by a number of regular regiments. "Let my men through...," demanded Roosevelt. When they saw that the Rough Riders intended to charge, the black troops of the Ninth and Tenth Regiments, as well as others, eagerly joined the attack. "I waved my hat," said Roosevelt later, "and we went up the hill in a rush."

Two black soldiers threw down a fence so that Roosevelt, the only officer on horseback, could ride ahead. Watching from a distance, reporter Richard Harding Davis later wrote, "Roosevelt mounted

Black troops of the Ninth Cavalry were in the front of the charge up San Juan Hill.

23

high on horseback, and charging the rifle-pits at a gallop and quite alone, made you feel that you would like to cheer." Behind their colonel, the Rough Riders charged recklessly, shooting and running up the slope. "Yes, they were going up the hill, up the hill," exclaimed newspaperman Stephen Crane. "It was the best moment of anybody's life."

One bullet grazed Roosevelt's elbow. Near the summit, he sprang from his horse and climbed over a barbed-wire fence. Joining their colonel, the Rough Riders scrambled to the crest of Kettle Hill in the face of heavy enemy fire. As the wave of soldiers swarmed close, the frightened Spaniards threw down their guns and ran.

Kettle Hill was captured and the Rough Riders

The battle at Kettle Hill (left). Roosevelt (right) was the only Rough Rider on horseback.

cheered. To the left, Roosevelt saw other U.S. troops storming San Juan Hill. "Obviously," the colonel remembered, "the proper thing to do was to help them." Fiercely Roosevelt yelled for his troops to join in the charge. "Thinking that the men would all come," he recalled, "I jumped over the wire fence in front of us and started at the double . . . . After running about a hundred yards I found I had only five men along with me."

With bullets whizzing around him, Roosevelt raced back to Kettle Hill. "We didn't hear you, we didn't see you go, Colonel," honestly exclaimed his surprised soldiers. "Lead on now," they promised, "we'll sure follow you." Together with the black and

U.S. soldiers capture San Juan Hill.

white troops from other regiments, the Rough Riders attacked San Juan Hill. Overpowered, the Spaniards fled.

From the summit of conquered San Juan Hill, the Rough Riders cheered again. The battle for the San Juan Heights had cost the regiment eighty-six killed or wounded. But in the distance, the soldiers could see the rooftops of Santiago.

Nearly surrounded now, Admiral Pascual Cervera desperately tried to save his Spanish fleet. On the morning of July 3, 1898, Cervera's ships steamed out of Santiago Harbor. Aboard the *Brooklyn*, Commodore Winfield S. Schley promptly raised the U.S. signal flags: "Clear all ships for action. Engage the

enemy." The huge guns of the U.S. battleships thundered. Unable to escape, all of the Spanish ships were sunk, beached, or burning. The battle of Santiago was over.

The loss of the Spanish fleet ended Spanish control of Santiago and all of Cuba. While surrender talks took place, the American soldiers cautiously waited atop San Juan Heights. Every day, rainstorms drenched the unsheltered troops. Often, food supplies ran low. Wet and hungry men fell sick of tropical diseases, and many died. And hidden in the nearby jungle Spanish snipers fired deadly bullets into the American lines. Determined to stop

The naval battle in Santiago Harbor. The Spanish fleet under Admiral Cervera (inset, left) was defeated by American forces under Commodore Schley (inset, right).

the snipers, Colonel Roosevelt picked a group of the best marksmen among the Rough Riders. The sharpshooters crawled into the jungle and silenced the enemy. Rough Rider James C. Goodwin, an Arizona rancher, shot down six Spanish snipers in a single afternoon.

On the morning of July 17, bugles sounded along the American lines. Santiago had surrendered. The Rough Riders gleefully threw their hats in the air. "At last, after seventeen days of fighting and waiting, the city is ours," said Rough Rider Ogden Wells. On August 12, Spain agreed to grant Cuba's independence, and also gave up the nearby island of Puerto Rico to the United States. In later arrangements the Philippines would come under American control for the next forty-eight years.

Outside Santiago, the American army waited for new orders. Finally, Roosevelt wrote an urgent letter to the War Department. He described the danger of yellow fever if the army remained encamped in Cuba. Within days the troops boarded ships in Santiago and gladly started for home.

The *Miami* carried the Rough Riders north. It docked at Montauk, Long Island, New York, on August 15, 1898. "Roosevelt! Roosevelt! Hurrah for Teddy and the Rough Riders!" roared the crowd. Lean and sunburned, the Rough Riders marched down the gangway. A band played patriotic tunes, people waved flags, and deafening cheers filled the air. "Oh, but we have had a bully fight!" Roosevelt

Color Sergeant Wright holds the battle-tattered flag of the Rough Riders.

joyfully declared. In less than four months the United States had won its war with Spain. This swift victory secured the United States a place among the world's great powers.

On September 13, just 133 days after it was formed, the First Volunteer Cavalry Regiment disbanded at Camp Wykoff on Long Island. The ranchers and Indians started their long dusty journey home to the Western territories. Wealthy New Yorkers went back to their mansions and private clubs, and some Ivy Leaguers got back to their colleges in time to start the new school year.

It was over. But few Americans will ever forget the Rough Riders. Their daring charge up San Juan

Colonel Roosevelt (center) and the Rough Riders at the point where they charged over the hill at San Juan

Hill had thrilled the nation. It also made Theodore Roosevelt a national hero. The Rough Rider colonel was elected governor of New York and then vice-president of the United States of America. When President McKinley was assassinated in September 1901, Roosevelt was thrust into the White House as the nation's twenty-sixth president. When he was elected in his own right in 1904, many Rough Rider veterans rode in his inaugural parade. Surely they remembered 1898 and Roosevelt's tearful farewell when he told his men: "I would honestly rather have my position as colonel of this regiment than any other position on earth." The bonds of deepest comradeship would hold the Rough Riders together forever. The record of their brave deeds has echoed down through history.

President Theodore Roosevelt delivered his inaugural address (left) on March 4, 1905. Roosevelt's exploits with the Rough Riders helped to advance his political career.

31

Colonel Roosevelt's farewell to the Rough Riders

INDEX

About the Author

Zachary Kent grew up in Little Falls, New Jersey. He is a graduate of St. Lawrence University and holds a teaching certificate in English. Following college he was employed at a New York City literary agency for two years until he decided to launch a career as a writer. To support himself while writing, he has worked as a taxi driver, a shipping clerk, and a house painter.

Mr. Kent has had a lifelong interest in American history. As a boy the study of the United States presidents was his special hobby. His collection of presidential items includes books, pictures, and games, as well as several autographed letters.